CW00867978

Copyright © 2019 Shaaron Fedora.

Interior Image Credit: Kezzia Crossley

All rights reserved. No part of this book may be used or reproduced by any means, graphic, electronic, or mechanical, including photocopying, recording, taping or by any information storage retrieval system without the written permission of the author except in the case of brief quotations embodied in critical articles and reviews.

Balboa Press books may be ordered through booksellers or by contacting:

Balboa Press
A Division of Hay House
1663 Liberty Drive
Bloomington, IN 47403
www.balboapress.com
1 (877) 407-4847

Because of the dynamic nature of the Internet, any web addresses or links contained in this book may have changed since publication and may no longer be valid. The views expressed in this work are solely those of the author and do not necessarily reflect the views of the publisher, and the publisher hereby disclaims any responsibility for them.

Any people depicted in stock imagery provided by Getty Images are models, and such images are being used for illustrative purposes only. Certain stock imagery © Getty Images.

ISBN: 978-1-9822-2255-0 (sc)
ISBN: 978-1-9822-2254-3 (e)

Library of Congress Control Number: 2019902138

Print information available on the last page.

Balboa Press rev. date: 02/27/2019

**BALBOA.**
PRESS
A DIVISION OF HAY HOUSE

# JEMMA
## The Most Wondering Angel

Shaaron Fedora

Illustrated by Kezzia Crossley

For the Earth Family

Sometimes we wonder
why things happen
the way they do

FYI

Here is what happened
and why

In the vastness of the endless Universe
there is not
there never was
and may never be
an Angel more enchanting
than the Angel they call
JEMMA.

# JEMMA
enchanted everyone she met

Her joy could not be contained
within her Angel heart

It spilled over into the Heavens
It made the stars twinkle as she passed by

She was just that kind of Angel.

While other Angels strolled quietly
through meadows filled with wild flowers

JEMMA

spun and twirled and danced among them

JEMMA

was an Angel Prima Ballerina.

The other Angels loved to watch
JEMMA
pirouette and spin about the heavens

I think she even danced in her dreams
because she was often seen
napping on a fluffy cloud
wearing her tutu.

Every day as danced in the sunlight
and every night as she danced
among the stars and around the moon

JEMMA
wondered about all the wonderful things
she came upon.

She wondered about the sun and what makes it so warm
She wondered about rainbows
where they come from and where they go
She wondered what makes it rain and who makes the flowers
She wondered where butterflies sleep
She wondered what makes colors shimmer
in the sunlight

She wondered


and wondered


and wondered.

All the Angels said that
JEMMA
was the Most Wondering Angel
in all the Heavens

If she was on one star and saw
another star over there
she rushed off to see that star too

If she was dancing under a beautiful rainbow
and saw another rainbow in the distance
off she went to see that rainbow.

JEMMA
never stayed long in one place.

There was always something more to see
Something more to do
Something more to know.

One fine day while Jemma was pirouetting
about the Heavens
she came upon a brilliant, blue jewel
way off in space

It was just there ... all alone

It was so magnificent it took her breath away.

Jemma stopped mid-pirouette to gaze at it
She gazed at it for a long long time
It truly was the most beautiful thing
she had ever seen

"What is it?" she whispered in awe.

She was told it was Planet Earth and that
some day
when she was ready
she would go there.

Everything changed

From that moment on
JEMMA
spent a lot of time gazing at
the brilliant jewel called Planet Earth

She thought about it a lot
She dreamed about it a lot

"What's it like," she wondered.
"Can I go and see it?"

The Council of Angels knew that
Jemma was not ready
It wasn't her time

But Jemma was very inquisitive
and very persistent and
she just had to go there

Jemma pleaded.

"I won't stay long," she promised.
"I'll come right back.
I just want to see it.
I need to see it."

Everyone told Jemma
there was only one way to Planet Earth
and that was with a family

She would need a family

What's more
she would need a family that would be willing
to let her return to Heaven
right after she got there.

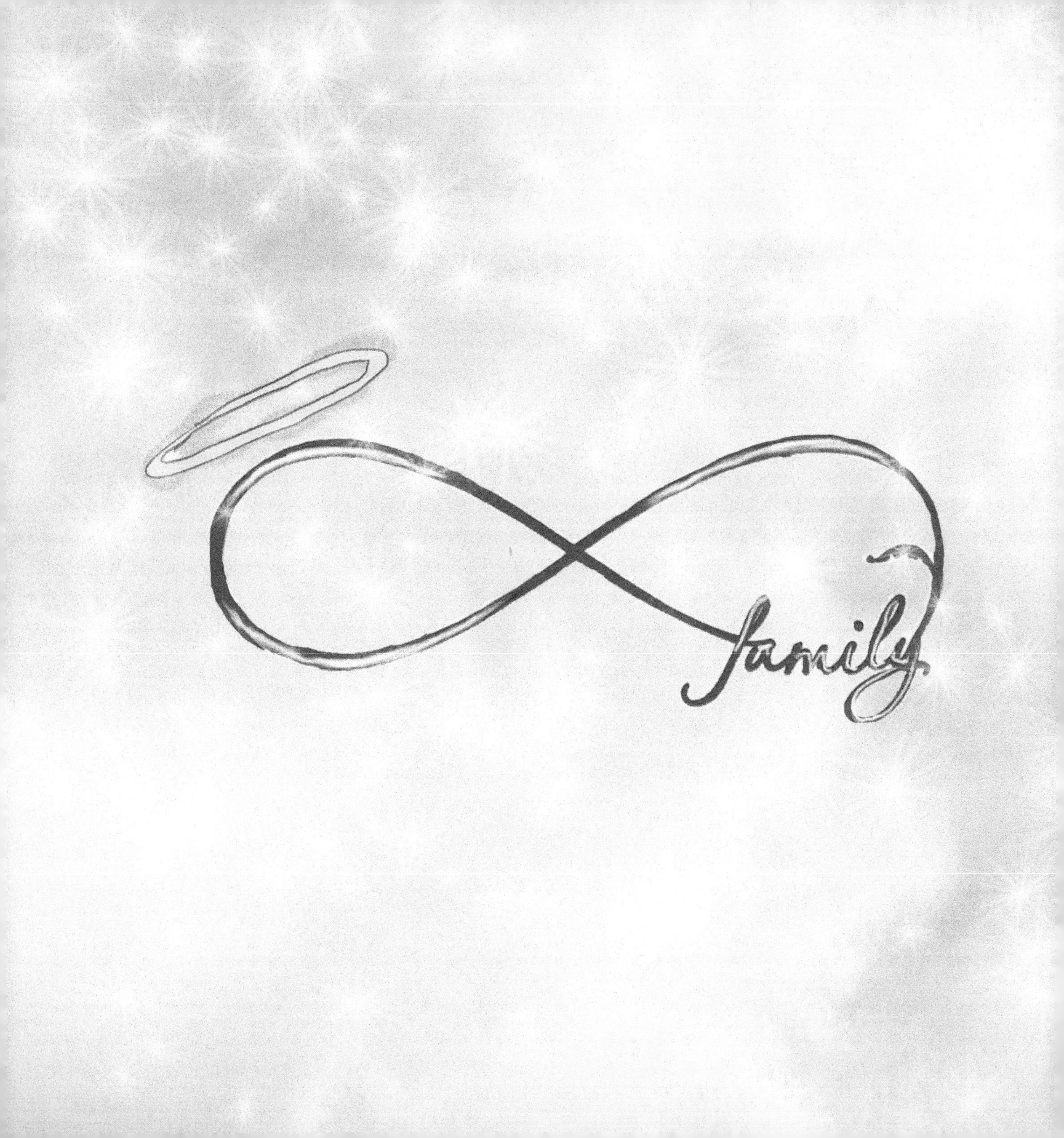
family

All the grown up Angels told Jemma
it would not be easy to find
the kind of family she would need

A Family
brave enough
and strong enough
and
who would love her enough
to let her go

She would need to find a very Special Family.

JEMMA
was undaunted

She would search far and wide

To the ends of the Earth
if need be

She just had to find her Special Family

And that was that!

Jemma started searching right away

She would find a Mommy and a Daddy
who would love her forever

Even though
she would stay with them for only
a brief moment

Even though
they would be very sad when she left.

Jemma didn't dance about
about the Heavens as much anymore

She spent most of her days

And her nights
way past bedtime

Searching for her Special Family

Searching
and
Searching.

Finally
she found them

Her little heart just about burst

The family
had a Mommy and a Daddy
and even more it had a Sister

Jemma knew for sure this was her Family
because the Sister had a tutu just like hers

She presented her Special Family
to the Council of Angels and they were approved.

And so it came to pass


On a warm day in spring
JEMMA
arrived on Planet Earth


She stayed only a moment
Just like she promised


Then she went back to Heaven.

JEMMA
has now seen the beautiful jewel
called Planet Earth


and


she now has an Earth Family all her own.

Someday they will meet again
until then. . . .


JEMMA
watches over her Family from Heaven above


They will be her Family for all eternity
she will love them forever
and
she is forever grateful to them
for giving her
the precious gift of Planet Earth.

If you look up at the sky on a warm night
and see the stars twinkling
JEMMA
is there dancing among them

If you stand very still and close your eyes
and really believe
you will feel her love
touch your cheek
as she sprinkles stardust down upon you.

And that's the story of
JEMMA
The Most Wondering Angel
who still dances among the stars.

And that's what really happened.
I got it from a reliable source.

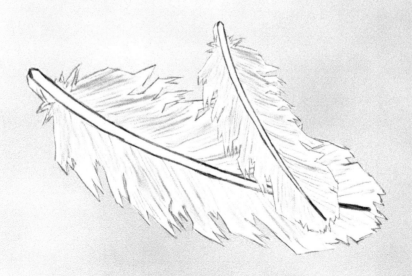

CPSIA information can be obtained
at www.ICGtesting.com
Printed in the USA
BVHW021225080319
542164BV00028B/1395/P